# HEALING YOUR LOST CHILD

"A Journey to Wholeness and Self-Acceptance

*A Step-by-Step Guide to Healing Trauma and Embracing Your Authentic Self*

By Anns Bell

All rights reserved. No part of this publication may be reproduced, distributed, or transmitted in any form or by any means, including photocopying, recording, or other electronic or mechanical methods, without the prior written permission of the publisher, except in the case of brief quotations embodied in critical reviews and certain other noncommercial uses permitted by copyright law.

Copyright © Anns Bell , 2023.

## Table of Contents

Chapter 1: Understanding The Concept of the Inner Child and Its Role in Adult Life.

Chapter 2: Recognizing The Signs of a Wounded Inner Child

Chapter 3: Exploring The Causes and Origins of Inner Child Trauma

Chapter 4: Understanding The Connection Between the Inner Child and Addiction

Chapter 5: Exploring The Impact of Childhood Conditioning On Adult Relationships

Chapter 6: Techniques for Healing and Nurturing the Inner Child

Chapter 7: Mindfulness and Self-Compassion in Inner Child Healing

Chapter 8: Identifying and Releasing Repressed Emotions and Past Traumas

Chapter 9: Building A Healthy Inner Parent and Learning to Set Boundaries

Chapter 10: Re-Parenting the Inner Child and Building a Positive Inner Narrative

Chapter 11: Incorporating Play and Creativity into Inner Child Healing

Chapter 12: The Role of Therapy and Professional Support in Inner Child Healing

Chapter 13: Understanding The Role of Spirituality in Inner Child Healing

Chapter 14: Overcoming Resistance and Obstacles in Inner Child Healing

Chapter 15: Integrating The Healed Inner Child into Daily Life and Relationships.

Chapter 16: Case Studies and Personal Stories of Healing Journey

Chapter 17: Conclusion

## **Personal Story**

I never really understood the concept of the inner child until I hit rock bottom. I had always been a high achieving, successful individual, but inside I felt empty and unfulfilled. I had buried my past traumas and repressed emotions so deep that I didn't even realize they existed. But, as it turns out, they were still very much present, affecting my thoughts, my behaviors, and my relationships.

It all came to a head when my marriage fell apart, and I found myself alone and lost. That's when I started to seek help and discovered the concept of the inner child. I learned that my inner child was wounded and that I needed to heal it in order to move forward in my life.

The first step was to identify my repressed emotions and past traumas. I started by journaling and writing down any memories that came to mind. I also started to practice mindfulness and meditation to help me be more present and aware of my thoughts and feelings. Through this process, I was able to uncover a lot of repressed emotions and past traumas that I had not fully acknowledged or processed.

The next step was to release these repressed emotions and past traumas. I began working with a therapist who specialized in inner child healing, and we used a variety of techniques such as cognitive-behavioral therapy, trauma-focused therapy, emotion-focused therapy, and play therapy. These techniques helped me to process and heal from my past traumas and to release my repressed emotions.

One of the most challenging parts of the process was learning to forgive myself and others. I had spent so much time blaming myself and others for my wounds that I didn't realize how much it was holding me back. But as I began to understand that everyone does the best they can with the resources they have, I was able to let go of the past and move on.

I also learned the importance of building a healthy inner parent. I visualized and imagined a nurturing and supportive inner parent, and it helped me to feel safe and secure. I also learned to set boundaries and communicate in a clear and assertive way, this helped me to promote self-care and improve overall well-being.

Through this process, I was able to heal my inner child and to build a positive inner narrative. I was able to let go of the past and move forward in my life. I felt happier, more fulfilled and more confident in myself and my abilities.

It wasn't an easy journey, but it was definitely worth it. I realized that healing the inner child is an ongoing process, and I continue to work on it every day. I would encourage anyone who is struggling to take the first step and seek help. You don't have to go through it alone, and healing is possible.

# Chapter 1: Understanding The Concept of the Inner Child and Its Role in Adult Life.

The concept of the inner child refers to the emotional and psychological aspect of a person that remains childlike and innocent. This inner child is believed to hold the memories, feelings, and experiences that we had as children and that continue to shape our thoughts, emotions, and behavior as adults.

The inner child is often associated with the emotional baggage that we carry from our childhood, such as traumas, fears, and limiting beliefs. These negative experiences can cause the inner child to become wounded and as a result, it can affect adult life in many ways. For example, it can lead to feelings of anxiety, depression, and low self-worth. It can also manifest in unhealthy coping mechanisms such as addiction, self-sabotage, and lack of boundaries.

The concept of the inner child has its roots in psychoanalysis, specifically in the work of Carl Jung, who believed that the psyche is made up of different parts, including the conscious and unconscious mind, and the childlike part of the psyche which he referred to as the "child archetype." This child archetype represents the innate potential and creativity that we have within us, but it can also be influenced by the experiences and emotions of our childhood.

In the 1980s, psychotherapist John Bradshaw popularized the term "inner child" and brought it into mainstream consciousness. He emphasized the importance of understanding the inner child in the context of adult emotional healing and personal growth. He believed that the inner child holds the key to understanding our emotional baggage and that healing the inner child can help us to overcome limiting beliefs and patterns of behavior that can hold us back in life.

When the inner child is wounded, it can lead to a wide range of emotional and psychological issues in adulthood. For example, a child who has experienced neglect or abandonment may grow into an adult who has difficulty trusting others or forming healthy relationships. A child who has been emotionally or physically abused may grow into an adult who struggles with self-worth and self-esteem.

The inner child can also play a role in the development of mental health issues such as anxiety and depression. When traumatic experiences are not properly processed and integrated, they can lead to the formation of negative beliefs and patterns of behavior that can contribute to the development of mental health issues.

It's important to note that not all emotional baggage is a result of childhood traumas, some of it can be accumulated through the course of life, but understanding and healing the inner child can help in resolving those issues as well.

However, it's important to remember that the inner child also holds the key to our potential, our creativity, and our ability to experience joy and wonder. When the inner child is nurtured and healed, it can have a positive impact on our self-esteem, relationships, and overall well-being.

Understanding the concept of the inner child and its role in adult life is crucial for personal growth and self-awareness. It allows us to gain insight into the patterns of behavior and thoughts that may be holding us back and to tap into the positive aspects of our inner child. This can help us to overcome limiting beliefs and to become more authentic, resilient, and fulfilled.

Healing the inner child can be a challenging and emotional process, but it's worth it. It involves exploring our childhood experiences, identifying the negative beliefs and patterns that have developed as a result, and learning new ways of coping with and processing emotions. It also involves learning how to nurture and care for the inner child, which can include activities such as journaling, meditation, and creative expression.

It's also important to understand that healing the inner child is not just about resolving past traumas but also about learning to live in the present.

## Chapter 2: Recognizing The Signs of a Wounded Inner Child

Recognizing the signs of a wounded inner child is crucial for understanding the emotional baggage that may be holding us back in life and for taking steps to heal and nurture the inner child. Some common signs of a wounded inner child include:

**Difficulty with trust and relationships:** A wounded inner child may have difficulty trusting others and forming healthy relationships as a result of past traumas such as neglect or abandonment.

**Low self-esteem and self-worth:** A wounded inner child may struggle with feelings of worthlessness and inadequacy, which can be the result of past emotional or physical abuse.

**Difficulty with emotional regulation:** A wounded inner child may struggle with managing emotions, resulting in outbursts of anger, anxiety, or depression.

**Difficulty in setting boundaries:** A wounded inner child may have difficulty saying "no" and setting healthy boundaries, which can result in feelings of being overwhelmed and resentful.

**Difficulty in dealing with criticism:** A wounded inner child may have a hard time receiving criticism, feeling hurt and defensive.

**Difficulty in dealing with change:** A wounded inner child may have a hard time adapting to new situations, feeling anxious and uncomfortable.

**Difficulty in dealing with stress:** A wounded inner child may have a hard time coping with stress, resorting to unhealthy coping mechanisms such as addiction or self-sabotage.

**Difficulty in dealing with rejection:** A wounded inner child may have a hard time dealing with rejection and may become overly attached to people and things.

**Difficulty in dealing with abandonment:** A wounded inner child may have a hard time dealing with abandonment and may become overly attached to people and things.

**Difficulty in dealing with success:** A wounded inner child may have a hard time dealing with success, feeling guilty or unworthy.

It's important to note that not everyone will experience all of these signs and some people may experience different signs that aren't listed here. However, recognizing these signs can be a helpful starting point for understanding the emotional baggage that may be holding us back in life and for taking steps to heal and nurture the inner child.

It's also important to note that not all of these signs are necessarily a direct result of a wounded inner child, and can be a symptom of other underlying issues as well.

However, understanding the role of the inner child in our emotional lives can help in identifying and resolving these issues.

Recognizing the signs of a wounded inner child can be a difficult and emotional process, but it's an important step in the journey of healing and self-discovery. By understanding the root causes of our emotional baggage and the patterns of behavior that may be holding us back in life, we can take steps to heal and nurture the inner child.

This can include activities such as journaling, meditation, therapy, and creative expression. It can also involve learning how to set healthy boundaries, how to deal with difficult emotions, and how to develop self-compassion and self-acceptance.

Ultimately, recognizing the signs of a wounded inner child is about understanding and embracing our authentic selves, and taking steps to heal and nurture the inner child. This can lead to a greater sense of self-awareness, self-acceptance, and fulfillment in life.

# Chapter 3: Exploring The Causes and Origins of Inner Child Trauma

Exploring the causes and origins of inner child trauma is an important step in understanding and healing the emotional baggage that may be holding us back in life. Trauma can take many forms and can occur at any age, but childhood traumas often have a particularly deep and lasting impact on the inner child.

**Some common causes and origins of inner child trauma include:**

**Childhood abuse:** Physical, emotional, or sexual abuse can have a profound and lasting impact on the inner child. The trauma of abuse can lead to feelings of worthlessness, low self-esteem, and difficulty in trusting others. It can also lead to difficulty in dealing with difficult emotions and can manifest in unhealthy coping mechanisms such as addiction, self-sabotage, and lack of boundaries.

**Neglect**: Neglect can be just as damaging as abuse and can lead to similar emotional and psychological issues. The inner child may struggle with feelings of worthlessness and a lack of self-worth, as well as difficulty in forming healthy relationships.

**Loss:** The loss of a parent, sibling, or other loved one can have a deep and lasting impact on the inner child. The trauma of loss can lead to feelings of abandonment, difficulty in dealing with rejection, and difficulty in adapting to new situations.

**Trauma in the family:** Trauma within the family, such as domestic violence, can have a deep and lasting impact on the inner child. The trauma can lead to feelings of fear, anxiety, and a lack of safety.

**Bullying:** Being bullied as a child can have a deep and lasting impact on the inner child. The trauma can lead to feelings of worthlessness, low self-esteem, and difficulty in dealing with criticism.

**Divorce:** The trauma of divorce can have a deep and lasting impact on the inner child. The trauma can lead to feelings of abandonment, difficulty in dealing with change, and difficulty in forming healthy relationships.

**Natural disasters:** Natural disasters such as hurricanes, earthquakes, and floods can have a deep and lasting impact on the inner child. The trauma can lead to feelings of fear, anxiety, and a lack of safety.

It's important to note that these are just some examples of the causes and origins of inner child trauma, and that everyone's experiences will be unique. It's also important to note that not all traumas are as obvious or severe as those listed here, and that some traumas may be more subtle or may be the result of a combination of factors.

It's also important to note that not all of these causes are necessarily direct causes of inner child trauma, and may be causes of other underlying issues as well. However, understanding the role of the inner child in our emotional lives can help in identifying and resolving these issues.

Exploring the causes and origins of inner child trauma can be a difficult and emotional process, but it is necessary for healing and self-discovery. By understanding the root causes of our emotional baggage and the patterns of behavior that may be holding us back in life, we can take steps to heal and nurture the inner child.

This can include activities such as journaling, meditation, therapy, and creative expression. It can also involve learning how to set healthy boundaries, how to deal with difficult emotions, and how to develop self-compassion and self-acceptance.

It's also important to understand that exploring the causes and origins of inner child trauma is not about blame or placing fault on someone else or ourselves. It's about understanding and accepting our past experiences and using that understanding to move forward in a positive way.

Ultimately, exploring the causes and origins of inner child trauma is about understanding and embracing our authentic selves.

## Chapter 4: Understanding The Connection Between the Inner Child and Addiction

Understanding the connection between the inner child and addiction is an important aspect of inner child healing. Addictions can be a way for individuals to cope with unresolved emotional pain and trauma from their past. The inner child, which holds these unresolved emotions and traumas, can play a significant role in the development and maintenance of addiction.

Research has shown that childhood trauma, such as abuse, neglect, and abandonment, can increase the risk of developing addiction later in life. These traumatic experiences can lead to emotional pain, feelings of worthlessness, and a lack of self-worth, which can be numbed and temporarily relieved through the use of substances or other addictive behaviors.

Additionally, individuals who experienced childhood trauma may not have had a supportive and nurturing inner parent to provide guidance, protection, and support. Without this inner parent, they may struggle to regulate their emotions and may turn to addiction as a form of self-soothing.

Furthermore, addiction can also be a form of self-punishment for repressed emotions and past traumas. People may feel guilty or ashamed about their past and turn to addiction as a way to punish themselves for their perceived shortcomings.

It's important to note that addiction is a complex issue, and addressing the connection between the inner child and addiction requires a holistic approach. This may involve therapy, inner child healing practices, and professional support to address the underlying emotional pain and traumas.

One approach is to use cognitive-behavioral therapy, trauma-focused therapy, emotion-focused therapy, and play therapy to help individuals identify and process repressed emotions and past traumas, and to develop a healthy inner parent. This can help individuals to feel safe and secure, and to regulate their emotions in a healthy way.

Another approach is to use mindfulness and meditation to help individuals be more present and aware of their thoughts and feelings, and to learn to accept and process them in a healthy way.

Additionally, it's important to incorporate self-compassion and forgiveness in the healing process. These practices can help individuals to let go of blame and resentment, and to develop a positive inner narrative.

It's important to note that healing from addiction and inner child healing is a personal and individual process, and there is no one-size-fits-all approach. It's essential to find a method that works best for you.

## Chapter 5: Exploring The Impact of Childhood Conditioning On Adult Relationships

Exploring the impact of childhood conditioning on adult relationships is an important aspect of inner child healing. Childhood conditioning refers to the beliefs, attitudes, and behaviors that are learned and internalized during childhood, and can have a significant impact on adult relationships.

One of the most significant ways that childhood conditioning can impact adult relationships is through the development of attachment patterns. Attachment patterns refer to the way in which individuals form and maintain relationships and are often formed in childhood through interactions with primary caregivers. If an individual had a supportive and nurturing relationship with their primary caregivers, they are more likely to form healthy attachment patterns in adulthood. However, if an individual had a traumatic or neglectful relationship with their primary caregivers, they may struggle to form healthy attachment patterns in adulthood.

For example, individuals who experienced neglect or abandonment in childhood may develop an avoidant attachment pattern in adulthood, characterized by a fear of intimacy and a tendency to push others away. They may struggle to trust others and may have difficulty forming close relationships. On the other hand, individuals who experienced abuse in childhood may develop an anxious attachment pattern in adulthood, characterized by a need for constant reassurance and a fear of rejection. They may struggle with feelings of insecurity and may have difficulty trusting others.

Additionally, childhood conditioning can also impact adult relationships through the development of negative self-beliefs and self-worth. If an individual experienced neglect, abandonment, or abuse in childhood, they may develop negative self-beliefs such as "I'm not good enough" or "I'm not worthy of love." These negative self-beliefs can impact adult relationships by leading to feelings of insecurity, self-doubt, and a fear of rejection.

Furthermore, childhood conditioning can also impact adult relationships through the development of unhealthy coping mechanisms. For example, if an individual experienced neglect or abandonment in childhood, they may develop unhealthy coping mechanisms such as addiction, eating disorders, or self-harm as a way to cope with unresolved emotional pain. These coping mechanisms can further impact adult relationships by leading to feelings of guilt, shame, and self-loathing.

It's important to note that childhood conditioning is not an excuse for unhealthy or destructive behavior in adult relationships. However, understanding the impact of childhood conditioning can help individuals to address and overcome these issues.

One approach is to work with a therapist or counselor who is trained in inner child healing and attachment theory. They can help individuals to identify and process repressed emotions and past traumas and to develop a healthy inner parent. This can help individuals to feel safe and secure, and to regulate their emotions in a healthy way.

# Chapter 6: Techniques for Healing and Nurturing the Inner Child

Healing and nurturing the inner child is an important step in overcoming emotional baggage and living a more authentic and fulfilled life. There are a variety of techniques that can be used to heal and nurture the inner child, some of which include:

**Journaling:** Journaling is a powerful tool for healing and nurturing the inner child. It is a form of self-expression that allows us to explore and understand our thoughts, feelings, and experiences in a safe and non-judgmental way.

One way to use journaling to heal and nurture the inner child is to write a letter to the inner child. This letter can be a way to express love, understanding, and acceptance to the inner child, and can also be used to address any specific issues or traumas that may be holding the inner child back.

Another way to use journaling to heal and nurture the inner child is to keep a journal specifically for the inner child. This journal can be used to express feelings and emotions, to document progress and growth, and to reflect on past experiences and traumas.

Journaling can also be used to identify patterns of behavior and thought that may be holding the inner child back in life. By writing down thoughts and feelings, it is possible to identify negative patterns of thought and behavior, and to develop new strategies for coping with difficult emotions and experiences.

Journaling can also be used to practice self-compassion and self-acceptance, which are essential for healing and nurturing the inner child. By being kind and understanding towards the inner child in the journal, one can develop a sense of self-compassion and self-acceptance, and learn to treat oneself with love and kindness.

Using prompts and reflective questions can also be helpful in journaling for inner child healing. Some examples of prompts are:

· What did you feel when you were a child in that situation?

· What do you need to hear from me right now?

· What do you wish you could tell your younger self?

It's important to remember that journaling is a personal and individual process, and there is no one-size-fits-all approach.

**Mindfulness and meditation:** Mindfulness and meditation can be powerful tools for healing and nurturing the inner child. Mindfulness practices, such as deep breathing, can help to calm the mind and reduce feelings of anxiety and stress. Meditation can help to develop self-compassion and self-awareness, which are essential for healing the inner child.

Mindfulness and meditation are powerful tools for healing and nurturing the inner child. They can help to calm the mind, reduce feelings of anxiety and stress, and develop self-compassion and self-awareness.

Mindfulness is the practice of being present and fully engaged in the current moment, without judgment. It can be practiced through simple exercises such as deep breathing, body scanning, or mindful walking. The purpose of mindfulness practice is to bring awareness to one's thoughts, emotions, and physical sensations in the present moment, with the goal of increasing self-awareness and reducing stress.

Meditation is a practice that involves focusing the mind on a specific object, thought, or activity to achieve a mentally clear and emotionally calm state. There are different forms of meditation such as mindfulness meditation, guided meditation, and visualization. The goal of meditation is to achieve a state of deep relaxation and inner peace, which can help to reduce stress and anxiety, as well as promote feelings of well-being.

When it comes to inner child healing, mindfulness and meditation can be used to develop ==self-compassion== and ==self-awareness==. By being present and non-judgmental towards the inner child, one can learn to ==treat oneself with kindness, understanding,== and ==compassion==. This can help to reduce feelings of worthlessness, low self-esteem, and difficulty in trusting others.

Mindfulness and meditation can also help to identify patterns of behavior and thought that may be holding the inner child back in life. By bringing awareness to one's thoughts and emotions, it is possible to identify negative patterns of thought and behavior, and to develop new strategies for coping with difficult emotions and experiences.

One specific form of mindfulness meditation that can be helpful in inner child healing is called "inner child meditation." This type of meditation involves visualizing the inner child and speaking to it with love, compassion, and understanding. This can help to heal past traumas and provide emotional support for the inner child.

It's important to note that mindfulness and meditation are personal and individual practices, and there is no one-size-fits-all approach. The most important thing is to find a technique that works for you, and to make time for regular practice. Mindfulness and meditation can be done in short intervals, even a few minutes a day, and gradually increase the duration as you get comfortable with the practice.

**Creative expression:** Creative expression, such as art, music, or writing, can be a powerful tool for healing and nurturing the inner child. Engaging in creative activities can help to tap into the childlike part of the psyche, which is associated with our innate potential and creativity. It can also help to process and make sense of difficult emotions and experiences.

Creative expression, such as art, music, writing, or dance, can be a powerful tool for healing and nurturing the inner child. Engaging in creative activities can help to tap into the childlike part of the psyche, which is associated with our innate potential and creativity. It can also help to process and make sense of difficult emotions and experiences.

Art therapy, for instance, is a form of therapy that uses art materials and the creative process to express emotions and feelings, explore personal issues, and promote healing and growth. Art therapy is based on the idea that the creative process can be therapeutic and can help individuals to communicate thoughts and feelings that may be difficult to express through words.

Writing therapy, also known as journal therapy or bibliotherapy, is a form of therapy that uses writing as a tool for self-expression and personal growth. Writing therapy can be used to explore thoughts, feelings, and experiences, to process and make sense of difficult emotions, and to promote self-awareness and self-compassion.

Music therapy is a form of therapy that uses music and its elements to promote healing and growth. Music therapy can be used to explore thoughts, feelings, and experiences, to process and make sense of difficult emotions, and to promote self-awareness and self-compassion.

Dance and movement therapy is a form of therapy that uses movement and dance to promote emotional, social, cognitive, and physical well-being. Dance and movement therapy can be used to explore thoughts, feelings, and experiences, to process and make sense of difficult emotions, and to promote self-awareness and self-compassion.

Creative expression can also be used to identify patterns of behavior and thought that may be holding the inner child back in life. By expressing oneself creatively, one can explore and understand the root causes of emotional baggage, and develop new strategies for coping with difficult emotions and experiences.

Creative expression can also be used to practice self-compassion and self-acceptance, which are essential for healing and nurturing the inner child. By expressing oneself creatively, one can learn to treat oneself with love and kindness. This can help to reduce feelings of worthlessness, low self-esteem, and difficulty in trusting others.

It's important to note that creative expression is a personal and individual process, and there is no one-size-fits-all approach. The most important thing is to find a form of creative expression that resonates with you and to make time for regular practice.

In summary, creative expression can be a powerful tool for healing and nurturing the inner child. Engaging in activities such as art therapy, writing therapy, music therapy, dance and movement therapy can help to tap into the childlike part of the psyche, process and make sense of difficult emotions, and promote self-awareness, self-compassion, and self-acceptance. It's a form of self-expression that allows us to explore and understand our thoughts, feelings, and experiences in a safe and non-judgmental way.

**Play:** Play is an essential aspect of healing and nurturing the inner child. Engaging in playful activities, such as sports, games, and hobbies, can help to tap into the childlike part of the psyche, which is associated with our innate potential and creativity. Play can also help to reduce stress and anxiety and promote feelings of joy and well-being.

Play is an essential aspect of healing and nurturing the inner child. Engaging in playful activities, such as sports, games, and hobbies, can help to tap into the childlike part of the psyche, which is associated with our innate potential and creativity. Play can also help to reduce stress and anxiety and promote feelings of joy and well-being.

Play therapy is a form of therapy that uses play as a medium for communication and expression. Play therapy can be used to explore thoughts, feelings, and experiences, to process and make sense of difficult emotions, and to promote self-awareness and self-compassion. Play therapy can be beneficial for children, adolescents, and adults and can be adapted to suit different age groups and needs.

Child-centered play therapy is a type of play therapy that focuses on the child's needs and interests. The therapist provides a safe and accepting environment where the child can express themselves freely and authentically. Through play, the child can explore and make sense of their experiences, feelings, and thoughts, and learn new ways of coping with difficult situations.

Sandplay therapy is a form of play therapy that uses a sandbox and miniature figures to create a symbolic representation of the child's inner world. The child can create scenes that reflect their current emotional state, experiences, and conflicts. By playing with the sand and figures, the child can process and make sense of their experiences in a safe and non-threatening way.

Games and sports can also be used as a form of play therapy. Games and sports can provide an outlet for stress and anxiety, and promote feelings of joy and well-being. They can also be used to promote teamwork, trust, and communication.

Hobbies and leisure activities such as gardening, cooking, or crafts, can also be used as a form of play therapy. These activities can provide an outlet for stress and anxiety and promote feelings of joy and well-being. They can also be used to promote self-expression, self-care, and relaxation.

It's important to note that play is a personal and individual process, and there is no one-size-fits-all approach. The most important thing is to find a form of play that resonates with you and to make time for regular practice. Play can be done in short intervals, and gradually increase the duration as you get comfortable with the activity.

In summary, play is an essential aspect of healing and nurturing the inner child. Engaging in playful activities such as play therapy, child-centered play therapy, sandplay therapy, games, sports, hobbies, and leisure activities can help to tap into the childlike part of the psyche, reduce stress and anxiety, and promote feelings of joy and well-being. Play can also be used to explore thoughts, feelings, and experiences, to process and make sense of difficult emotions, and to promote self-awareness, self-compassion and self-acceptance.

**Therapy:** Therapy can be a powerful tool for healing and nurturing the inner child. A therapist can help to explore and understand the root causes of emotional baggage, as well as provide tools and strategies for coping with difficult emotions and experiences. A therapist can also help to identify patterns of behavior and thought that may be holding you back in life.

Therapy is a powerful tool for healing and nurturing the inner child. A therapist can help to explore and understand the root causes of emotional baggage, as well as provide tools and strategies for coping with difficult emotions and experiences. A therapist can also help to identify patterns of behavior and thought that may be holding you back in life.

There are various forms of therapy that can be used to heal and nurture the inner child, some of which include:

***Cognitive-behavioral therapy (CBT):*** CBT is a form of therapy that focuses on the relationship between thoughts, feelings, and behavior. It can be used to identify and change negative patterns of thought and behavior that may be holding the inner child back in life. CBT can also be used to teach coping skills and develop a sense of self-compassion and self-acceptance.

***Trauma-focused therapy:*** Trauma-focused therapy is a form of therapy that specifically addresses the impact of trauma on the inner child. This type of therapy can be used to process and make sense of difficult experiences and emotions, and to develop coping skills and resilience.

***Eye Movement Desensitization and Reprocessing (EMDR):*** EMDR is a form of therapy that uses a combination of eye movements, sounds, or taps to help process traumatic memories and reduce the distress associated with them.

***Emotion-focused therapy:*** Emotion-focused therapy is a form of therapy that focuses on helping individuals to understand, accept, and regulate their emotions. This type of therapy can be used to develop self-compassion and self-acceptance, and to improve the ability to cope with difficult emotions.

***Family therapy:*** Family therapy is a form of therapy that involves the whole family. It can be used to identify and address patterns of behavior and thought that may be holding the inner child back in life. Family therapy can also be used to promote communication, understanding, and healing within the family.

***Play therapy:*** Play therapy is a form of therapy that uses play as a medium for communication and expression. Play therapy can be used to explore thoughts, feelings, and experiences, to process and make sense of difficult emotions, and to promote self-awareness and self-compassion.

It's important to note that therapy is a personal and individual process, and there is no one-size-fits-all approach. The most important thing is to find a therapist that you feel comfortable with and to make time for regular sessions. It's also important to remember that healing takes time and effort, and it's not a linear process. It's essential to have patience and compassion for oneself throughout the journey.

In summary, therapy is a powerful tool for healing and nurturing the inner child. A therapist can help to explore and understand the root causes of emotional baggage, as well as provide tools and strategies for coping with difficult emotions and experiences. Therapy can also be used to identify patterns of behavior and thought that may be holding you back in life. There are various forms of therapy, such as cognitive-behavioral therapy, trauma-focused therapy, EMDR, emotion-focused therapy, family therapy, and play therapy that can be used to heal and nurture the inner child. It's important to find a therapist that you feel comfortable with and to make time for regular sessions.

**Re-parenting:** Re-parenting is a therapeutic technique that involves learning to take care of the inner child in the way that it needed to be taken care of in childhood. This can include learning to set healthy boundaries, developing self-compassion and self-acceptance, and providing emotional support for the inner child.

Re-parenting is a technique for healing and nurturing the inner child that involves creating a new, healthy parent-child relationship within oneself. This technique can be used to address unresolved emotional issues and traumas from childhood and to provide the inner child with the love, understanding, and support that it may have missed in the past.

Re-parenting involves recognizing the inner child's needs and wants and providing them with the emotional support and guidance that is needed. It also involves learning to set boundaries and to provide discipline in a loving and compassionate way.

One of the key components of re-parenting is learning to be a "good enough" parent to oneself. This means learning to be patient, understanding, and non-judgmental towards the inner child. It also means learning to set boundaries and to provide discipline in a loving and compassionate way.

Another important aspect of re-parenting is learning to listen to the inner child. This can involve setting aside time to talk to the inner child and to hear its thoughts and feelings. It can also involve journaling or using other forms of creative expression to communicate with the inner child.

Re-parenting also involves learning to provide emotional support and guidance to the inner child. This can involve learning to set boundaries and to provide discipline in a loving and compassionate way. It can also involve learning to provide emotional support and guidance through self-compassion and self-acceptance.

Re-parenting can also involve learning to forgive oneself and one's parents for past mistakes. This can involve learning to let go of blame and to understand that everyone does the best they can with the resources they have.

Re-parenting techniques can be incorporated into other forms of therapy, such as cognitive-behavioral therapy, trauma-focused therapy, emotion-focused therapy, and play therapy. It can also be incorporated into journaling, mindfulness and meditation, and creative expression.

It's important to note that re-parenting is a personal and individual process, and there is no one-size-fits-all approach. It's essential to have patience and compassion for oneself throughout the journey. It is also important to work with a therapist or counselor who is trained in re-parenting techniques to guide you through the process.

In summary, re-parenting is a technique for healing and nurturing the inner child that involves creating a new, healthy parent-child relationship within oneself. It involves recognizing the inner child's needs and wants, providing emotional support and guidance, learning to set boundaries and discipline in a loving and compassionate way, learning to listen to the inner child, providing emotional support and guidance, learning to forgive oneself and one's parents for past mistakes, and incorporating re-parenting techniques into other forms of therapy. Re-parenting is a personal and individual process and it's important to work with a therapist or counselor who is trained in re-parenting techniques to guide you through the process.

**Body-based therapies:** Body-based therapies such as yoga, tai chi, and bodywork can be powerful tools for healing and nurturing the inner child. These therapies can help to release physical and emotional tension, promote feelings of relaxation and well-being, and improve overall physical health.

Body-based therapies are a form of healing that focus on the connection between the mind and body and can be an effective tool for healing and nurturing the inner child. These therapies include techniques such as yoga, mindfulness, and bodywork that help to release stored emotions and traumas, and promote a sense of well-being.

*Yoga* is a form of body-based therapy that involves physical postures, breathing exercises, and meditation. Yoga can help to release stored emotions and traumas and promote a sense of well-being. Yoga postures can also help to release tension and stress in the body and improve overall physical health. Yoga can also be used to develop self-compassion and self-acceptance and to promote a sense of inner peace and relaxation.

*Mindfulness* is a form of body-based therapy that involves paying attention to the present moment and being aware of one's thoughts and emotions. Mindfulness can help to release stored emotions and traumas and promote a sense of well-being. Mindfulness can also be used to develop self-compassion and self-acceptance and to promote a sense of inner peace and relaxation.

*Bodywork* is a form of therapy that involves working with the body to release stored emotions and traumas. Bodywork techniques such as massage, reflexology, and shiatsu can be used to release physical tension and promote a sense of well-being. Bodywork can also be used to develop self-compassion and self-acceptance and to promote a sense of inner peace and relaxation.

*Somatic therapy* is a form of therapy that focuses on the connection between the mind and body. Somatic therapy can help to release stored emotions and traumas and promote a sense of well-being. Somatic therapy can also be used to develop self-compassion and self-acceptance and to promote a sense of inner peace and relaxation.

It's important to note that body-based therapies are a personal and individual process, and there is no one-size-fits-all approach. The most important thing is to find a technique that works for you and to make time for regular practice. It's also important to work with a therapist or practitioner who is trained in body-based therapies to guide you through the process.

In summary, body-based therapies are a form of healing that focus on the connection between the mind and body and can be an effective tool for healing and nurturing the inner child. Techniques such as yoga, mindfulness, bodywork, and somatic therapy can help to release stored emotions and traumas, promote a sense of well-being, develop self-compassion and self-acceptance, and promote a sense of inner peace and relaxation. It's important to find a technique that works for you, make time for regular practice, and work with it.

**EFT tapping:** Emotional Freedom Technique (EFT) tapping is a type of psychological acupressure, based on the same energy meridians used in traditional acupuncture to treat physical and emotional ailments for over five thousand years, but without the invasiveness of needles. It has been shown to be effective in reducing symptoms of anxiety, PTSD and depression

EFT (Emotional Freedom Techniques) tapping, also known as tapping therapy, is a form of psychological acupressure that can be an effective tool for healing and nurturing the inner child. EFT tapping is based on the principle that negative emotions and physical pain are caused by disruptions in the body's energy system. By tapping on specific acupressure points on the body, EFT tapping can help to release the emotional blockages and restore the body's energy balance.

EFT tapping is a simple process that involves tapping on specific acupressure points on the body while focusing on a specific issue or emotion. The tapping is done with the fingertips and can be done on oneself or with the guidance of a therapist. The tapping process is accompanied by verbal affirmations, which help to reinforce the positive changes that are being made.

EFT tapping can be used to address a wide range of issues, including anxiety, depression, trauma, and phobias. It can also be used to address specific issues related to the inner child, such as feelings of worthlessness, low self-esteem, and difficulty in trusting others.

One of the key benefits of EFT tapping is that it can help to release stored emotions and traumas that may be holding the inner child back in life. By tapping on specific acupressure points and focusing on the issue, EFT tapping can help to release the emotional blockages and restore the body's energy balance.

EFT tapping can also be used to develop self-compassion and self-acceptance. By tapping on specific acupressure points and focusing on positive affirmations, EFT tapping can help to reinforce positive changes in self-perception and self-worth.

EFT tapping can also be used to promote a sense of inner peace and relaxation. By tapping on specific acupressure points and focusing on positive affirmations, EFT tapping can help to release stress and tension and promote a sense of well-being.

It's important to note that EFT tapping is a personal and individual process, and there is no one-size-fits-all approach. The most important thing is to find a therapist or practitioner who is trained in EFT tapping to guide you through the process. It's also important to be consistent with the practice.

**Gratitude journaling:** Keeping a gratitude journal can help to shift focus from negative thoughts and emotions to positive ones. It can also help to promote feelings.

Gratitude journaling is a powerful technique for healing and nurturing the inner child. It involves regularly taking the time to reflect on and write down things that you are grateful for in your life. This practice can help to shift focus from negative thoughts and emotions to positive ones and can promote feelings of well-being and inner peace.

Gratitude journaling can be done in a variety of ways. Some people prefer to write in a physical journal, while others prefer to use a digital journal or an app. The key is to find a method that works best for you and to make time for regular journaling.

One of the key benefits of gratitude journaling is that it can help to shift focus from negative thoughts and emotions to positive ones. By regularly reflecting on and writing down things that you are grateful for, you can change your perspective and start to see the positive aspects of your life. This can help to reduce feelings of stress, anxiety, and depression and promote feelings of well-being and inner peace.

Gratitude journaling can also be used to develop self-compassion and self-acceptance. By regularly reflecting on and writing down things that you are grateful for, you can start to appreciate yourself and your life. This can help to reduce feelings of worthlessness, low self-esteem, and difficulty in trusting others.

Gratitude journaling can also be used to promote a sense of inner peace and relaxation. By regularly reflecting on and writing down things that you are grateful for, you can start to release stress and tension and promote a sense of well-being.

To get started with gratitude journaling, you can begin by writing down three things that you are grateful for every day. You can also write down things that you are looking forward to, or things that you accomplished during the day. As you get comfortable with the practice, you can increase the number of things that you write down and also expand the scope of what you are grateful for.

It's important to note that gratitude journaling is a personal and individual process, and there is no one-size-fits-all approach. The most important thing is to find a method that works best for you and to make time for regular journaling. It's also important to be consistent with the practice, even on days when you may not feel like doing it. With time, you'll start to notice the positive impact that gratitude journaling can have on your life and on your inner child.

In summary, gratitude journaling is a powerful technique for healing and nurturing the inner child. It involves regularly taking the time to reflect on and write down things that you are grateful for in your life. This practice can help to shift focus from negative thoughts and emotions to positive ones, promote feelings of well-being and inner peace, develop self-compassion and self-acceptance.

## Chapter 7: Mindfulness and Self-Compassion in Inner Child Healing

Mindfulness and self-compassion are essential components of inner child healing. Mindfulness is the practice of being present and aware of one's thoughts, emotions, and physical sensations in the present moment. Self-compassion is the practice of treating oneself with kindness, care, and understanding, rather than judgment or criticism. Together, mindfulness and self-compassion can help to promote healing and growth for the inner child.

Mindfulness can be practiced in various ways, such as through meditation, yoga, and body awareness exercises. When applied to inner child healing, mindfulness can help to bring awareness to the inner child's thoughts, emotions, and physical sensations, which can help to release stored emotions and traumas. Mindfulness can also help to promote self-compassion by reducing negative self-talk and promoting a sense of self-awareness.

Self-compassion can also be practiced in various ways, such as through self-compassionate meditation, self-compassionate journaling, and self-compassionate self-talk. When applied to inner child healing, self-compassion can help to provide the inner child with a sense of safety and security, which can help to release stored emotions and traumas. Self-compassion can also help to reduce negative self-talk and promote self-awareness.

Mindfulness and self-compassion can also be applied to specific issues related to the inner child. For example, if the inner child is struggling with feelings of worthlessness, self-compassionate journaling or self-compassionate self-talk can be used to address these issues. If the inner child is struggling with low self-esteem, mindfulness and self-compassionate meditation can be used to address these issues.

It's important to note that mindfulness and self-compassion are personal and individual practices, and there is no one-size-fits-all approach. The most important thing is to find a method that works best for you and to make time for regular practice. It's also important to work with a therapist or counselor who is trained in mindfulness and self-compassion to guide you through the process.

In summary, Mindfulness and self-compassion are essential components of inner child healing. Mindfulness is the practice of being present and aware of one's thoughts, emotions, and physical sensations in the present moment. Self-compassion is the practice of treating oneself with kindness, care, and understanding, rather than judgment or criticism. Together, mindfulness and self-compassion can help to promote healing and growth for the inner child by providing a sense of safety, security, and self-compassion and reducing negative self-talk and promoting self-awareness, and by addressing specific issues related to the inner child.

# Chapter 8: Identifying and Releasing Repressed Emotions and Past Traumas

Identifying and releasing repressed emotions and past traumas is an essential step in the inner child healing process. Repressed emotions and past traumas can prevent individuals from living a fulfilling and happy life, and can prevent the inner child from healing.

Repressed emotions are emotions that an individual has not fully acknowledged or processed. They are often buried deep within the subconscious mind and can manifest in the form of negative thoughts, behaviors, and emotions. These repressed emotions can include anger, sadness, fear, guilt, and shame.

Past traumas are experiences that have caused emotional pain and have not been fully processed. These traumas can include childhood abuse, neglect, abandonment, or any other life events that have caused emotional pain.

To identify repressed emotions and past traumas, it's essential to be willing to examine one's past and to be open to the possibility that there may be unresolved issues. Journaling, mindfulness and meditation, creative expression, and play can be helpful in identifying repressed emotions and past traumas.

Releasing repressed emotions and past traumas can be done through a variety of techniques, such as cognitive-behavioral therapy, trauma-focused therapy, emotion-focused therapy, and play therapy. These techniques can help individuals to process and heal from the past traumas, and to release repressed emotions.

Releasing repressed emotions and past traumas can also involve learning to forgive oneself and others, and learning to let go of blame and resentment. This can involve learning to understand that everyone does the best they can with the resources they have, and learning to let go of the past and move on.

Additionally, it can be helpful to work with a therapist or counselor who is trained in inner child healing and in addressing repressed emotions and past traumas. They can provide guidance, support, and tools to help individuals process and heal from their past traumas and release repressed emotions.

It's important to note that identifying and releasing repressed emotions and past traumas is a personal and individual process, and there is no one-size-fits-all approach. It's essential to be open and honest with oneself and to be patient and compassionate throughout the process. It's also important to work with a therapist or counselor who is trained in inner child healing and in addressing repressed emotions and past traumas to guide you through the process.

In summary, identifying and releasing repressed emotions and past traumas is an essential step in the inner child healing process. Repressed emotions and past traumas can prevent individuals from living a fulfilling life.

# Chapter 9: Building A Healthy Inner Parent and Learning to Set Boundaries

Building a healthy inner parent and learning to set boundaries are important aspects of inner child healing. The inner parent is the part of the inner self that provides guidance, protection, and support for the inner child. A healthy inner parent can help to promote healing and growth for the inner child, while an unhealthy inner parent can prevent the inner child from healing.

The inner parent can be developed through a variety of techniques, such as visualization, guided imagery, and affirmations. Visualization and guided imagery can involve creating a mental image of a nurturing and supportive inner parent, and can be used to promote a sense of safety and security for the inner child. Affirmations can involve repeating positive statements to oneself, such as "I am a loving and supportive inner parent."

Another important aspect of inner child healing is learning to set boundaries. Setting boundaries involves learning to say "no" when necessary, and learning to communicate one's needs and wants in a clear and assertive way. This can help to promote self-care and can improve overall well-being.

Boundary setting also includes learning to be aware of our own needs and feelings, and also learning to respect the boundaries of others. This can be achieved through learning assertive communication, learning to say no and learning to respect the boundaries of others.

It's important to note that building a healthy inner parent and learning to set boundaries is a personal and individual process, and there is no one-size-fits-all approach. It's essential to find a method that works best for you and to make time for regular practice. It's also important to work with a therapist or counselor who is trained in inner child healing to guide you through the process.

In summary, building a healthy inner parent and learning to set boundaries are important aspects of inner child healing. A healthy inner parent can help to promote healing and growth for the inner child, while an unhealthy inner parent can prevent the inner child from healing. Building a healthy inner parent can be done through visualization, guided imagery, and affirmations. Setting boundaries involves learning to say "no" when necessary, and learning to communicate one's needs and wants in a clear and assertive way, learning to be aware of our own needs and feelings, and also learning to respect the boundaries of others. It's important to note that building a healthy inner parent and learning to set boundaries is a personal and individual process, and it's essential to work with a therapist or counselor who is trained in inner child healing to guide you through the process.

## Chapter 10: Re-Parenting the Inner Child and Building a Positive Inner Narrative

Re-parenting the inner child is a technique for healing and nurturing the inner child that involves creating a new, healthy parent-child relationship within oneself. This technique can be used to address unresolved emotional issues and traumas from childhood and to provide the inner child with the love, understanding, and support that it may have missed in the past. Building a positive inner narrative is also crucial in this process.

Re-parenting involves recognizing the inner child's needs and wants and providing them with the emotional support and guidance that is needed. It also involves learning to set boundaries and to provide discipline in a loving and compassionate way. Additionally, building a positive inner narrative means becoming aware of the negative self-talk and replacing it with positive affirmations that align with the person you want to be and the life you want to live.

One of the key components of re-parenting is learning to be a "good enough" parent to oneself. This means learning to be patient, understanding, and non-judgmental towards the inner child. It also means learning to set boundaries and to provide discipline in a loving and compassionate way. Building a positive inner narrative means learning to talk to yourself in a kind and supportive way and reminding yourself of your capabilities and strengths.

Another important aspect of re-parenting is learning to listen to the inner child. This can involve setting aside time to talk to the inner child and to hear its thoughts and feelings. It can also involve journaling or using other forms of creative expression to communicate with the inner child. Building a positive inner narrative means being attentive to the thoughts and feelings of the inner child and addressing them in a constructive way.

Re-parenting also involves learning to provide emotional support and guidance to the inner child. This can involve learning to set boundaries and to provide discipline in a loving and compassionate way. It can also involve learning to provide emotional support and guidance through self-compassion and self-acceptance. Building a positive inner narrative means developing a sense of self-worth and understanding that you are enough, and that you deserve love and happiness.

Re-parenting can also involve learning to forgive oneself and one's parents for past mistakes. This can involve learning to let go of blame and to understand that everyone does the best they can with the resources they have. Building a positive inner narrative means learning to forgive yourself and others, and to move on from past mistakes and traumas.

Re-parenting techniques can be incorporated into other forms of therapy, such as cognitive-behavioral therapy, trauma-focused therapy, emotion-focused therapy, and play therapy. It can also be incorporated into journaling, mindfulness and meditation, and creative expression. Building a positive inner narrative means incorporating positive affirmations and self-talk into these techniques.

It's important to note that re-parenting and building a positive inner narrative is a personal and individual process, and there is no one-size-fits-all approach. It's essential to have patience and compassion for oneself throughout the journey. It is also important to work with a therapist or counselor who is trained in re-parenting techniques and building a positive inner narrative to guide you through the process.

# Chapter 11: Incorporating Play and Creativity into Inner Child Healing

Incorporating play and creativity into inner child healing is an effective technique for addressing unresolved emotional issues and traumas from childhood. Play and creativity can provide a safe and non-threatening way for the inner child to express itself and to process difficult emotions. This can help to promote healing and growth for the inner child.

Play therapy is a form of therapy that uses play to communicate with and help children and inner child. Play therapy can help the inner child to express emotions and feelings that may be difficult to put into words. It can also help to provide a sense of safety and security and to promote self-awareness and self-compassion.

Creative expression, such as art, writing, music, and drama, can also be used to help the inner child express itself and process difficult emotions. Creative expression can provide a non-threatening way for the inner child to express itself and can be a powerful tool for healing and growth.

Incorporating play and creativity into inner child healing can also involve using fantasy and imagination. This can be done through guided imagery, visualization, and other techniques that allow the inner child to explore its emotions and feelings in a safe and non-threatening way.

Play and creativity can also be used to promote self-compassion and self-acceptance. By creating a safe and non-threatening environment for the inner child to express itself, play and creativity can help the inner child to develop a sense of self-worth and to understand that it is worthy of love and happiness.

It's important to note that incorporating play and creativity into inner child healing is a personal and individual process, and there is no one-size-fits-all approach. The most important thing is to find a form of play or creativity that resonates with you and to make time for regular practice. It's also important to work with a therapist or counselor who is trained in play and creativity-based therapies to guide you through the process.

In summary, incorporating play and creativity into inner child healing is an effective technique for addressing unresolved emotional issues and traumas from childhood. Play therapy, creative expression, and using fantasy and imagination can provide a safe and non-threatening way for the inner child to express itself and to process difficult emotions, which can help to promote healing and growth for the inner child. It can also promote self-compassion, self-acceptance and self-worth. It's important to find a form of play or creativity that resonates with you, make time for regular practice, and work with a therapist or counselor who is trained in play and creativity-based therapies.

## Chapter 12: The Role of Therapy and Professional Support in Inner Child Healing

The role of therapy and professional support in inner child healing is crucial. Inner child healing is a complex and often emotional process, and it can be difficult to navigate alone. A trained therapist or counselor can provide guidance, support, and tools to help individuals address unresolved emotional issues and traumas from childhood, and to promote healing and growth for the inner child.

Therapy can take many forms, but some of the most effective types of therapy for inner child healing include cognitive-behavioral therapy (CBT), trauma-focused therapy, emotion-focused therapy, and play therapy.

**Cognitive-behavioral therapy (CBT)** is a form of therapy that focuses on the relationship between thoughts, emotions, and behaviors. CBT can be used to help individuals change negative thought patterns and beliefs that may be preventing inner child healing. It can also be used to teach coping skills and to promote self-compassion and self-acceptance.

**Trauma-focused therapy** is a form of therapy that is specifically designed to address unresolved emotional issues and traumas from childhood. Trauma-focused therapy can be used to help individuals process and heal from traumatic events, and to promote healing and growth for the inner child.

**Emotion-focused therapy** is a form of therapy that focuses on helping individuals understand and accept their emotions. Emotion-focused therapy can be used to help individuals develop emotional regulation skills and to promote self-compassion and self-acceptance.

**Play therapy** is a form of therapy that uses play to communicate with and help children and inner child. Play therapy can help the inner child to express emotions and feelings that may be difficult to put into words. It can also help to provide a sense of safety and security and to promote self-awareness and self-compassion.

Another crucial aspect of inner child healing is working with a professional who understands the complexities of inner child healing and can provide guidance and support throughout the process. A therapist or counselor who is trained in inner child healing can provide guidance, support, and tools to help individuals address unresolved emotional issues and traumas from childhood, and to promote healing and growth for the inner child.

It's important to note that therapy and professional support are personal and individual processes, and there is no one-size-fits-all approach. It's essential to find a therapist or counselor who is trained in inner child healing and with whom you feel comfortable working. It's also important to be open and honest with your therapist or counselor and to be consistent with therapy sessions.

In summary, therapy and professional support play a crucial role in inner child healing. Working with a trained therapist or counselor can provide guidance, support, and tools to help individuals address unresolved emotional issues and traumas from childhood, and to promote healing and growth for the inner child. Therapy can take many forms, such as cognitive-behavioral therapy, trauma-focused therapy, emotion-focused therapy and play therapy.

## Chapter 13: Understanding The Role of Spirituality in Inner Child Healing

Understanding the role of spirituality in inner child healing can be an important aspect of the healing journey. Spirituality can be defined as an individual's sense of connection to something greater than themselves, and can include religious beliefs, practices, or a sense of purpose and meaning.

Spirituality can play a role in inner child healing by providing individuals with a sense of hope, peace, and purpose. It can also help individuals to make sense of their past traumas and to find meaning in their pain. Additionally, spirituality can also provide individuals with a sense of connection to something greater than themselves, which can help to reduce feelings of isolation and loneliness.

One way that spirituality can be incorporated into inner child healing is through the practice of mindfulness and meditation. Mindfulness is the practice of being present and aware of one's thoughts, emotions, and surroundings, and can be a powerful tool for inner child healing. It can help individuals to connect with their inner selves, to process and release repressed emotions, and to build a sense of inner peace.

Another way that spirituality can be incorporated into inner child healing is through the practice of gratitude. Gratitude is the practice of being thankful for what one has and can be a powerful tool for inner child healing. It can help individuals to shift their focus from their pain and suffering to the blessings and positive aspects of their lives.

Additionally, spirituality can also be incorporated into inner child healing through the practice of forgiveness. Forgiveness is the practice of letting go of resentment and anger towards oneself or others and can be a powerful tool for inner child healing. It can help individuals to release past traumas and to find peace and healing.

For some individuals, spirituality may also involve religious or spiritual practices such as prayer, ritual, or community. These practices can provide individuals with a sense of connection to something greater than themselves, and can provide comfort and support during the healing journey.

It's important to note that spirituality is a personal and individual experience, and what works for one person may not work for another. It's essential to find a spiritual practice that resonates with you and that feels authentic to you.

In summary, understanding the role of spirituality in inner child healing can be an important aspect of the healing journey. Spirituality can play a role in inner child healing by providing individuals with a sense of hope, peace, and purpose.

# Chapter 14: Overcoming Resistance and Obstacles in Inner Child Healing

Overcoming resistance and obstacles in inner child healing can be a challenging but essential part of the healing process. Inner child healing is a complex and often emotional process, and it can be difficult to navigate alone. Many individuals may experience resistance or obstacles that can prevent them from making progress in their healing journey.

One common form of resistance in inner child healing is denial. Denial is the act of refusing to acknowledge or accept the reality of a situation or an emotion. It can be a defense mechanism that prevents individuals from facing difficult emotions and traumas from their past. Overcoming denial can involve learning to recognize and acknowledge one's emotions and experiences, and learning to accept that they are real and valid.

Another form of resistance in inner child healing is fear. Fear can manifest in many forms, such as fear of failure, fear of rejection, and fear of the unknown. It can prevent individuals from taking the necessary steps to heal their inner child. Overcoming fear can involve learning to understand and accept one's fears, and learning to take small and manageable steps towards healing.

A third form of resistance in inner child healing is the lack of self-compassion. This can manifest in the form of negative self-talk, self-criticism, and low self-esteem. This can prevent individuals from being kind and compassionate towards themselves, and make it difficult for them to heal their inner child. Overcoming this form of resistance can involve learning to be self-compassionate, and to treat oneself with kindness and understanding.

A fourth form of resistance in inner child healing is the lack of trust in oneself and others. This can manifest in the form of difficulty in trusting others, difficulty in trusting oneself, and difficulty in trusting the healing process. It can prevent individuals from making progress in their healing journey. Overcoming this form of resistance can involve learning to trust oneself, learning to trust others, and learning to trust the healing process.

A fifth form of resistance in inner child healing is the lack of time or resources. This can manifest in the form of feeling overwhelmed with other responsibilities, or not having access to the necessary resources or support to heal. Overcoming this form of resistance can involve learning to make time for yourself.

## Chapter 15: Integrating The Healed Inner Child into Daily Life and Relationships.

Integrating the healed inner child into daily life and relationships is an important step in the inner child healing process. It involves integrating the lessons and insights gained from the healing process into one's daily life and relationships. This can help to promote healing and growth for the inner child and can improve overall well-being and happiness.

One important aspect of integrating the healed inner child into daily life is learning to set and maintain healthy boundaries. This involves learning to say "no" when necessary, and learning to communicate one's needs and wants in a clear and assertive way. This can help to promote self-care and can improve overall well-being.

Another important aspect of integrating the healed inner child into daily life is learning to practice self-compassion. This involves treating oneself with kindness, understanding, and forgiveness. It can also involve learning to practice self-compassion in daily life through self-compassionate self-talk and self-compassionate journaling.

It is also important to integrate inner child healing into relationships. This can involve learning to communicate in a clear and assertive way, learning to set and maintain healthy boundaries, and learning to practice self-compassion in relationships. It can also involve learning to forgive oneself and others, and learning to let go of blame and resentment.

Additionally, it is important to continue the inner child healing practice in daily life, this can be achieved through journaling, mindfulness and meditation, creative expression, and play. It can also involve working with a therapist or counselor who is trained in inner child healing to continue to provide guidance and support throughout the process.

It's important to note that integrating the healed inner child into daily life and relationships is a personal and individual process, and there is no one-size-fits-all approach. It's essential to find a method that works best for you and to make time for regular practice. It's also important to work with a therapist or counselor who is trained in inner child healing to guide you through the process.

In summary, integrating the healed inner child into daily life and relationships is an important step in the inner child healing process. It involves integrating the lessons and insights gained from the healing process into one's daily life and relationships, this can help to promote healing and growth for the inner child and can improve overall well-being and happiness. This can be achieved by setting and maintaining healthy boundaries, practicing self-compassion, and integrating inner child healing into relationships. Additionally, it is important to continue the inner child healing practice in daily life, this can be achieved through journaling, mindfulness and meditation, creative expression, and play, and working with a therapist or counselor who is trained in inner child healing to continue to provide guidance and support throughout the process.

# Chapter 16: Case Studies and Personal Stories of Healing Journey

One example of a case study is a woman named Sarah, who had a difficult childhood growing up with an abusive and neglectful parent. Throughout her adult life, Sarah struggled with feelings of worthlessness, guilt, and shame. She also had a hard time setting boundaries and expressing her needs in relationships.

Through therapy and inner child healing practices, Sarah was able to identify and release repressed emotions and past traumas. She learned to set boundaries and communicate in a clear and assertive way. She also learned to practice self-compassion and to forgive her parent for the abuse and neglect she experienced. With the help of therapy, Sarah was able to develop a healthy inner parent and to build a positive inner narrative.

Another example is a man named John, who experienced abandonment from his mother in his childhood. He had a hard time trusting others and himself. He also had a hard time with forgiveness and letting go of resentment. Through therapy and inner child healing practices, John was able to identify and release repressed emotions and past traumas. He learned to trust himself and others, and to forgive his mother for abandoning him. He also learned to let go of resentment and to build a positive inner narrative.

These stories illustrate the different struggles and triumphs that individuals can experience during the inner child healing process. They also show that healing is possible, no matter how difficult the past may have been.

It's important to note that case studies and personal stories are not meant to be used as a substitute for professional therapy or guidance. They can, however, serve as a valuable source of inspiration and hope for readers who are on their own healing journey.

## Chapter 17: Conclusion

In conclusion, healing your lost inner child is a journey of self-discovery and self-care. It involves identifying and addressing repressed emotions and past traumas, and developing a positive inner narrative. The process can be challenging, but it is also incredibly rewarding as it allows individuals to find peace, happiness, and fulfillment in their lives.

The first step in healing your lost inner child is to identify and acknowledge repressed emotions and past traumas. This can be done through journaling, mindfulness, and meditation. It's important to understand that repressed emotions and past traumas do not define you and that healing is possible.

Once you have identified and acknowledged your repressed emotions and past traumas, the next step is to release them. This can be done through therapy, inner child healing practices, and professional support. These practices can help you to process and heal from your past traumas and to release your repressed emotions.

Another important aspect of inner child healing is to build a healthy inner parent. The inner parent is the internal representation of the caregiving figures in your life, and it can play a vital role in regulating emotions and promoting self-care.

Additionally, incorporating play and creativity, mindfulness and self-compassion, and therapy and professional support can be effective techniques in inner child healing.

It's important to note that healing the inner child is an ongoing process, and it's essential to have a support system in place to help you cope with triggers and flashbacks. It's also important to remember that everyone's healing journey is unique and that there is no one-size-fits-all approach.

In addition, understanding the role of spirituality in inner child healing can be an important aspect of the healing journey. Spirituality can provide individuals with a sense of hope, peace, and purpose and can be incorporated into inner child healing through practices such as mindfulness, gratitude, forgiveness, and prayer.

Furthermore, understanding the connection between inner child and addiction, childhood conditioning and adult relationships and also dealing with triggers and flashbacks are important aspect of inner child healing.

In conclusion, healing your lost inner child is a journey of self-discovery and self-care that requires patience, dedication, and support. But with the right tools and mindset, healing is possible, and individuals can find peace, happiness, and fulfillment in their lives.

**THE END**

Printed in Great Britain
by Amazon